CLAUDE ARTIFACT AI

Screenshots Transforming into Solutions

15 Practical Use Cases That Will Change How You Work with Artificial Intelligence

Kylan P.crook

Copyright © 2024 by Kylan P.crook

All rights reserved. No part of this publication may be reproduced, distributed, or transmitted in any form or by any means, including photocopying, recording, or other electronic or mechanical methods, without the prior written permission of the publisher, except in the case of brief quotations embodied in critical reviews and certain other noncommercial uses permitted by copyright law.

TABLE OF CONTENT

INTRODUCTION.. 3
Chapter 1: Getting Started with Claude Artifact.. 6
Chapter 3: Building Visual Charts and To-Do List Apps.. 23
Chapter 4: The Business Intelligence Dashboard... 32
Chapter 5: Real-Time Interactive Social Media Analyzer... 42
Chapter 6: Games and Learning Tools with Claude Artifact..................................... 51
Chapter 7: Advanced Features and Custom Dashboards.. 61
Chapter 8: Claude Artifact for Games and Fun.. 71
Chapter 9: Claude Projects: Maximizing Potential...81
Chapter 10: How Claude Artifact Will Change Your Workflow............................92
CONCLUSION...103

INTRODUCTION

Imagine a world where the power of complex software lies not in the hands of tech experts but in the fingertips of anyone with a simple idea. What if all you needed to create an interactive app, visualize complex data, or design a game was a screenshot and a few words? No coding, no advanced programming, just raw simplicity powered by the wonders of artificial intelligence. This is no fantasy; it's reality. This is Claude Artifact.

From the moment Claude Artifact hit the scene, it has redefined what's possible with AI. It bridges the gap between technical expertise and everyday creativity. Whether you're a business professional, an educator, or simply someone who loves tinkering with new tools, this technology is a game-changer. But here's the twist: while many are still fumbling with traditional software, you'll be ahead of the curve, wielding AI like a master. This book isn't just a guide—it's a key to unlocking the future of work and creativity, one Claude Artifact at a time.

But what makes Claude Artifact so special? In a sea of AI tools, how does it rise above? It's not just about generating code or building dashboards; it's about turning something as simple as a screenshot into a fully functional, shareable solution. Whether it's transforming raw data into a polished sales dashboard or bringing educational lessons to life with interactive tools, Claude Artifact puts the power of AI in your hands without asking you to understand the complexities behind it.

Throughout this book, you'll uncover fifteen revolutionary ways to use Claude Artifact. Each one more practical, more engaging, and more life-changing than the last. From visualizing data in ways that make presentations pop, to creating interactive apps in minutes, you'll discover how to turn mundane tasks into moments of innovation. This is not just about following a step-by-step guide—it's about transforming how you think about productivity, creativity, and problem-solving.

So, get ready. With every turn of the page, you'll venture deeper into the possibilities of what AI can do, not just for your work but for the way you approach challenges and ideas. The rules have changed, and by the end of this book, you'll not only understand those rules—you'll be rewriting them.

Chapter 1: Getting Started with Claude Artifact

- **What is Claude Artifact?**: Introduction to the tool, its purpose, and basic functionalities.
- **How to Activate Claude Artifact**: Step-by-step guide on turning on Claude Artifact for users.
- **First Look: Creating a Web App from a Screenshot**: Walkthrough of the very first use case - building a web app using a screenshot and a simple prompt

•

In an era where technology evolves at an unprecedented pace, finding tools that not only keep up with innovation but also democratize access to it is crucial. Enter Claude Artifact—an AI marvel that redefines how we interact with technology. Imagine a tool so intuitive that it transforms a mundane screenshot into a dynamic web app with nothing more than a few words of instruction. This is not science fiction but a groundbreaking reality made possible by Claude Artifact.

Claude Artifact represents a paradigm shift in how we engage with artificial intelligence. It's more than just a tool; it's a gateway to unleashing creativity and productivity without the complexities typically associated with tech development. At its essence, Claude Artifact serves a singular purpose: to simplify the creation of functional digital solutions from basic inputs. Whether you're envisioning an interactive dashboard, an educational tool, or a personalized application, Claude Artifact makes it accessible to anyone willing to explore its potential.

So, what exactly is Claude Artifact? In the landscape of AI tools, Claude Artifact stands out by providing a user-friendly interface that translates everyday digital tasks into actionable outputs. It eliminates the need for extensive coding knowledge by using sophisticated algorithms to interpret user inputs and generate relevant solutions. This could mean transforming a static image into an interactive web app or converting a basic dataset into a detailed, dynamic dashboard. It bridges the gap between conceptual ideas and tangible results, making sophisticated technology accessible to a broader audience.

Claude Artifact's magic begins with its activation. Unlike many advanced tools that require complicated setup procedures, Claude Artifact is designed with user convenience in mind. To activate Claude Artifact, you simply need to access your Claude AI account. Once logged in, the activation process is straightforward. Navigate to your profile icon, which directs you to a settings page. Here, under "Feature Preview," you will find the option to enable Claude Artifact. A quick toggle is all it takes to activate the feature. This simplicity is key—Claude Artifact is about efficiency and ease, ensuring that users can start exploring its capabilities with minimal fuss.

For many users, this seamless integration into existing workflows is a game-changer. Traditional software development often involves multiple steps, from installing programs to configuring environments. In contrast, Claude Artifact's activation process is designed to be intuitive and user-friendly, reflecting its core philosophy of accessibility. By minimizing setup complexities, Claude Artifact ensures that users can focus on their creative and practical goals without being bogged down by technical hurdles.

Once activated, Claude Artifact opens up a world of possibilities. The most compelling way to experience this is by diving into one of its fundamental use cases: creating a web app from a screenshot. Let's walk through this fascinating process. Picture this: you have a screenshot of a sales dashboard from your computer. The data is critical, but the image alone is static and lacks interactivity. You wonder if there's a way to make this visual data more dynamic and shareable. With

Claude Artifact, you can turn this screenshot into a functional web app with astonishing ease.

The process begins with uploading the screenshot into Claude Artifact's interface. This is where the tool's design simplicity shines. The interface is clean, with a focus on ease of use. You upload the image, and the next step is to provide a simple prompt. For instance, you might instruct Claude Artifact to "Create a web app using this image." This instruction is all it takes to set the AI into motion. Claude Artifact's sophisticated algorithms analyze the screenshot, generating the necessary code to create an interactive web application.

What's remarkable is how Claude Artifact abstracts away the complexity of coding. As the AI processes your prompt, it provides a live preview of the web app being created. This preview allows you to see how your static screenshot is being transformed into a functional application in real time. You don't need to understand the underlying code or programming languages. Instead, you're presented with a visually engaging result that you can interact with, modify, and publish.

The first time you witness this transformation, it's nothing short of magical. The tool takes what was once a mere image and turns it into a vibrant, interactive web app. You can further customize the app, adding features or modifying the layout according to your needs. This flexibility ensures that the final product aligns perfectly with your vision, whether it's a detailed sales dashboard or a simple interactive form.

Claude Artifact's capabilities extend beyond just creating web apps. Once you're familiar with the basics, you'll find that the tool is capable of much more. For instance, it can generate data visualizations from raw datasets, create interactive educational tools, and even design simple games. The process remains consistent: you provide an input, whether it's a screenshot, dataset, or text prompt, and Claude Artifact handles the complexity, delivering a polished, functional output.

One of the standout features of Claude Artifact is its ability to remix and share creations. After you've built your web app or interactive tool, you can publish it with a single click, generating a shareable link. This link allows others to view and interact with your creation. Even more exciting is the "remix" feature, which lets others take your app and build upon it. This collaborative aspect is particularly valuable in team settings or educational environments, where shared creativity and iterative development can lead to remarkable results.

As you delve deeper into using Claude Artifact, you'll discover that its power lies in its adaptability. The tool not only simplifies the creation process but also evolves with your needs. Each interaction with Claude Artifact refines its understanding of your requirements, making subsequent projects smoother and more intuitive. It's a testament to how AI can enhance creativity and productivity, not by replacing human ingenuity but by augmenting it.

In summary, Claude Artifact represents a significant leap forward in making advanced technology accessible and useful to a broader audience. Its ability to transform basic inputs into sophisticated digital solutions with minimal effort is a game-changer for anyone looking to innovate or streamline their work. By removing the barriers of traditional software development, Claude Artifact empowers users to focus on what truly matters: their ideas and creativity.

With Claude Artifact, the future of interactive applications, data visualization, and digital creativity is within reach. As you embark on this journey, you'll find that the tool's ease of use and powerful capabilities open up a world of possibilities, allowing you to turn everyday tasks into extraordinary achievements.

Chapter 2: The Power of Interactive Data

- **Creating Interactive Dashboards**: Explaining how to use Claude Artifact to build sales dashboards, including uploading CSV or PDF files to generate visualized data.
- **Sorting and Organizing Data**: Demonstrating how Claude Artifact automatically sorts data to create structured and interactive charts.
- **Case Study: Building a Sales Dashboard**: A detailed use case on turning sales data into an interactive dashboard for presentations.

Claude Artifact's true potential begins to shine when it comes to interactive data. In today's data-driven world, static information can only take you so far. Whether you're working in sales, marketing, education, or virtually any field, the ability to interact with data, to visualize trends, and to draw insights at a glance is invaluable. This is where Claude Artifact becomes indispensable, transforming raw information into something dynamic and alive. And it all starts with the creation of interactive dashboards.

Imagine you've got a large dataset sitting in a CSV file or a PDF report filled with raw sales figures. Traditionally, turning that data into a meaningful, visually engaging dashboard might require advanced knowledge of tools like Excel, Tableau, or even some programming languages. But with Claude Artifact, that process is not only simplified but also accelerated. You start by uploading the data directly into the platform. The interface is intuitive, allowing you to drag and drop files like CSVs or PDFs into the dashboard builder. What happens next feels almost magical.

Claude Artifact doesn't just display your data in a static format; it reads and interprets it, analyzing the structure and content of your file. Whether you're dealing with monthly sales reports, customer data, or financial trends, Claude Artifact sorts through the figures to identify the key metrics. It automatically organizes the data into a format that can be visualized in various ways—pie charts, line graphs, bar charts, and more—all without requiring any input from you beyond the initial file upload.

For instance, let's say you're uploading a CSV file containing last year's sales data. The columns list product names, sales figures, dates, and regions. Claude Artifact quickly recognizes this structure and begins to craft a dashboard that highlights the most important metrics: sales over time, product performance by region, and top-selling items. The software isn't just laying out your data in a grid; it's actively interpreting the information to create a compelling narrative that you can adjust and refine with just a few clicks. This is the true power of Claude Artifact—turning static data into something that tells a story.

The visualized data is interactive by nature. You can click on specific data points, drill down into individual months or products, and filter results based on various parameters. This interactivity is a game-changer in both presentations and day-to-day analysis. Instead of overwhelming your audience with raw numbers, you present a clean, professional dashboard where key insights are readily accessible. For sales teams, this means being able to present data that's not only easy to understand but also adaptive to the questions and focus areas of stakeholders. If a manager asks how a particular product performed in a specific region, you can filter the dashboard on the spot to show just that.

But Claude Artifact doesn't just stop at creating visually stunning dashboards. It goes a step further by automatically organizing and sorting your data. Once the raw information is uploaded, the tool begins to process it—sorting by dates, regions, product types, or whatever structure best suits the nature of your data. You don't need to manually enter formulas or adjust settings to organize it; Claude Artifact does the heavy lifting. For example, if your sales data includes figures for multiple regions over the course of a year, Claude Artifact will group the data into monthly or quarterly breakdowns and display it in a format that's easy to digest. The resulting dashboard is both functional and aesthetically pleasing, designed to maximize clarity while minimizing the time you spend on configuration.

This is where we dive into a specific case study: turning sales data into a dashboard for a major presentation. Let's say you're preparing for an annual meeting with your company's leadership team. You've been tasked with presenting a year-end sales report, and you need it to be more than just a series of slides with static numbers. You want the presentation to be interactive, visually engaging, and capable of answering spontaneous questions from the audience. With Claude Artifact, this becomes not only possible but remarkably easy.

You begin by gathering your sales data—perhaps it's stored in multiple CSV files from different departments, or maybe it's summarized in a lengthy PDF report. You upload these files into Claude Artifact, and within moments, the tool has sorted and organized the data, recognizing sales trends over time, highlighting which products performed the best, and even identifying regional differences in sales figures. The dashboard it generates is dynamic, allowing you to adjust the view in real-time. You can drill down into the specific sales performance of individual products, compare quarterly results, and even highlight anomalies or outliers in the data.

As you step into the presentation, instead of walking your audience through a series of dull spreadsheets, you now have an interactive dashboard that visually conveys the story of the year's sales performance. The leadership team can ask questions like, "How did product X perform in the European market compared to the previous quarter?" With a few clicks, you filter the dashboard to show just that, presenting data that's both specific and visually engaging. The ability to adapt the presentation on the fly adds a layer of sophistication and responsiveness that traditional slideshows or spreadsheets simply can't offer.

This case study highlights not only the tool's ease of use but also its ability to transform how we interact with data in real-time. Claude Artifact doesn't just present information; it gives you the tools to explore, question, and engage with the data in ways that were previously time-consuming and complex. By automating much of the data sorting and visualization process, it frees you to focus on the bigger picture: understanding and communicating the insights that matter most.

The benefits extend beyond just sales teams or corporate presentations. In any field where data plays a critical role, Claude Artifact becomes a powerful ally. Educators can use it to create interactive lesson plans based on student performance data, researchers can visualize their findings in real time, and marketing teams can track campaign performance with dashboards that update automatically. The versatility of the tool means that anyone with a dataset and a need for clarity can benefit from its capabilities.

The power of interactive data is more than just a convenience; it's a revolution in how we handle and present information. With Claude Artifact, the barriers to creating meaningful, dynamic dashboards are removed, empowering users to engage with their data in ways that lead to better insights and more informed decision-making. Whether you're preparing for a major presentation or simply trying to make sense of a large dataset,

Claude Artifact transforms the process into something intuitive, efficient, and, above all, interactive.

Chapter 3: Building Visual Charts and To-Do List Apps

- **Generating Visual Charts from Data**: How to create image-based charts for presentations and reports.
- **Building Simple To-Do List Apps**: Guide on using Claude Artifact to build functional to-do lists, including examples like the Microsoft To-Do list.
- **Use Case Breakdown: The Microsoft To-Do List Clone:** Storytelling example of replicating Microsoft To-Do in seven attempts using Claude Artifact.

Chapter 3 delves into the art of visual communication and simple task management, two areas where Claude Artifact truly excels. Data is only as good as the clarity with which it is presented, and when it comes to delivering insights in meetings or reports, visual charts are

23

indispensable. Likewise, staying organized is key in any professional setting, and creating functional apps like to-do lists is an everyday necessity. These two tasks—chart generation and to-do list building—are streamlined with Claude Artifact, offering an easy, efficient way to go from raw data and ideas to polished, usable outputs.

The process of generating visual charts from data is one of the most impressive and practical features of Claude Artifact. Traditionally, creating image-based charts requires multiple steps—whether it's copying data into software like Excel, manually creating graphs, or customizing chart elements to fit the style of your presentation. However, with Claude Artifact, the majority of this work is automated, allowing you to focus on the interpretation of the data rather than its presentation.

Imagine you're working on a quarterly sales report. You've got a table filled with data: product names, revenue, units sold, and growth percentages.

Typically, you'd need to either format the data yourself or send it to a design team to create visual charts for the final presentation. But Claude Artifact eliminates these extra steps. By simply uploading your data—whether it's in a CSV format, an Excel sheet, or even a table embedded within a PDF—Claude Artifact interprets the figures and suggests the best possible visualizations for your needs. It quickly generates line graphs, pie charts, bar graphs, and other chart types based on the data provided, and you have the ability to customize these charts to fit your specific preferences.

For instance, if your sales report includes data from different regions and you want to compare sales performance in North America versus Europe, Claude Artifact will generate side-by-side charts that allow for easy comparison. The software's ability to automatically format and style the charts based on the content ensures a professional finish that's ready for any presentation or report. What would have taken hours to create manually can now be completed in a matter of minutes, freeing you to spend more time analyzing the data itself and less time formatting it.

Beyond the automated creation of visual charts, Claude Artifact offers a surprising level of flexibility when it comes to chart design. If you're working on a marketing report and need charts that highlight campaign performance over time, you can adjust the colors, labels, and even chart types with just a few clicks. You can quickly switch between bar charts, line graphs, and scatter plots to see which format best conveys the message you're trying to deliver. This real-time adaptability is a powerful tool, especially when deadlines are tight, and you need to make last-minute adjustments.

The convenience of generating image-based charts is further enhanced by Claude Artifact's integration with other software platforms. For example, once your charts are created, you can easily export them into formats compatible with PowerPoint, Google Slides, or even directly into PDFs. This seamless integration ensures that your charts maintain their quality and formatting regardless of the platform you're using.

While visualizing data is one strength of Claude Artifact, its versatility extends to other practical applications, such as building functional to-do list apps. Staying organized is crucial, especially when juggling multiple tasks and deadlines. A simple, well-designed to-do list can make all the difference. Claude Artifact allows you to build your own customized to-do list apps with ease, ensuring that your personal or professional projects stay on track.

Take, for example, a common scenario: you're managing a team working on several simultaneous projects. Instead of relying on a generic app, you can use Claude Artifact to create a to-do list tailored to your team's specific needs. Start by defining the categories for tasks—perhaps by project name, priority level, or due date. Claude Artifact helps you build a functional, interactive app where tasks can be added, updated, or marked complete. You can set up notifications, assign tasks to different team members, and organize the to-do list by priority or deadline. The beauty of using Claude Artifact for this is that you don't need to have any coding experience to build these apps; the tool's user-friendly interface does the heavy lifting for you.

One of the most illustrative examples of Claude Artifact's capabilities in this area is building a Microsoft To-Do list clone. Microsoft To-Do is a popular app used by millions to manage their tasks, and replicating its functionality can seem like a complex challenge. However, Claude Artifact simplifies this process to the point where you can create a functional clone of the app in just a few steps. In this example, you would start by defining the core functions you want your to-do list app to have: task creation, prioritization, notifications, and completion tracking.

The process of replicating Microsoft To-Do using Claude Artifact is not only straightforward but also demonstrates the tool's power. After defining the basic parameters for your app, such as task categories and notifications, you would use Claude Artifact to automate much of the app-building process. Claude Artifact helps you design a sleek, intuitive interface where users can easily add tasks, set reminders, and mark items as complete. The final product is a functional to-do list app that rivals Microsoft To-Do in both design and usability, but with the added benefit of customization tailored specifically to your needs.

What makes this use case even more impressive is how quickly it can be achieved. Rather than taking weeks or months to design and develop a custom app, Claude Artifact allows you to build a functioning to-do list in just a few attempts. Each iteration refines the design and functionality until the final product meets your expectations. In just seven attempts, you could have an app that not only mimics the core features of Microsoft To-Do but also includes additional features tailored to your specific workflow.

The real strength of Claude Artifact lies in its ability to transform what might seem like complex tasks into manageable, accessible solutions. Whether it's creating visually stunning charts for your next presentation or building a simple to-do list app that helps you stay on top of your tasks, Claude Artifact's intuitive design and powerful automation features make it an indispensable tool.

In conclusion, Chapter 3 highlights the diverse capabilities of Claude Artifact, from turning raw data into beautiful, interactive visual charts to building fully functional to-do list apps. The power of automation and customization means that users can tackle a wide range of tasks without needing extensive technical skills. This chapter serves as a reminder that with the right tools, anyone can become a master of both data visualization and app development, making their work more efficient, organized, and professional.

Chapter 4: The Business Intelligence Dashboard

- **Understanding Business Intelligence**: Defining business intelligence and its importance in decision-making.
- **Creating a Business Intelligence Dashboard with Claude Artifact**: Step-by-step breakdown of generating a dashboard that includes sales performance, market share, and financial forecasts.
- **Case Study: Bringing a Presentation to Life**: Example of how an interactive business intelligence dashboard can replace traditional PowerPoint slides.

Business intelligence is at the core of effective decision-making in today's fast-paced business environment. It transforms raw data into actionable insights, allowing organizations to make informed decisions that drive growth, improve performance, and provide a competitive edge. As businesses generate vast amounts of data every day—from sales figures to market trends, and customer feedback—there's an increasing need for tools that can process this information quickly and accurately. Claude Artifact meets this need by offering a solution that can take large datasets and transform them into comprehensive, easy-to-understand business intelligence dashboards. This allows users to make data-driven decisions with confidence.

Business intelligence goes beyond just understanding the numbers. It's about identifying patterns, recognizing opportunities, and predicting future outcomes. With Claude Artifact, businesses can build interactive dashboards that give a real-time view of their key performance indicators (KPIs). These dashboards serve as a central hub for business data, consolidating sales performance, market share, financial forecasts, and more into one place. This not only saves time but also improves the quality of insights available, helping business leaders to make strategic decisions based on the most up-to-date information.

Let's explore how Claude Artifact simplifies the creation of a business intelligence dashboard, making the process accessible even to those without deep technical knowledge. Imagine you are a sales manager overseeing a team across multiple regions. You need a way to track performance metrics—how each region is performing, the overall sales numbers, market share, and projections for the next quarter. A traditional approach might involve piecing together various reports, manually updating spreadsheets, and presenting static PowerPoint slides in meetings. But with Claude Artifact, you can automate the entire process, creating a dynamic and interactive dashboard that updates in real-time as new data comes in.

The first step to creating a business intelligence dashboard with Claude Artifact is uploading the relevant data. Whether the information comes from spreadsheets, CSV files, or even cloud-based databases, Claude Artifact can quickly integrate this data and begin to visualize it in meaningful ways. As the data is uploaded, Claude Artifact interprets the numbers, organizing them into charts, graphs, and other visual formats that are most appropriate for the dataset.

For example, if you want to analyze regional sales performance, Claude Artifact might suggest a bar chart that shows how each region compares in terms of revenue. If you need to track market share over time, it might automatically generate a line graph that highlights trends in customer acquisition and retention.

Once the data is uploaded and visualized, the next step is customizing the dashboard to fit your specific needs. Claude Artifact provides an intuitive interface where you can adjust the layout, change chart types, and add filters to drill down into specific metrics. If you want to focus on performance in a particular region or time frame, you can easily toggle between different views. This flexibility ensures that the dashboard is not only visually appealing but also tailored to provide the exact insights you need.

Let's take a closer look at the key elements that might be included in a business intelligence dashboard built with Claude Artifact. Sales performance is often at the heart of any business intelligence system. Using Claude Artifact, you can generate a sales dashboard that shows revenue by product line, region, or sales team. The dashboard might include a pie chart showing how much each region contributed to total sales, alongside a bar graph that tracks revenue growth over time. You can also include KPIs such as average deal size, win rates, and sales cycle length, providing a comprehensive view of your sales performance.

Another essential component of a business intelligence dashboard is market share analysis.

Claude Artifact allows you to track how your company is performing relative to the competition, visualizing market share data in an easy-to-understand format. By combining sales data with market research, you can see where you're gaining or losing ground, helping to inform future marketing and sales strategies. For instance, you might find that your market share has increased in one region but stagnated in another. This insight allows you to take targeted action, such as increasing marketing efforts or reallocating resources to underperforming areas.

In addition to sales and market share, financial forecasts are a critical element of any business intelligence dashboard. Claude Artifact can integrate financial data, including revenue projections, expense trends, and profit margins, into the dashboard. This allows business leaders to not only see how the company is performing today but also anticipate future financial outcomes. The dashboard might feature a graph that projects revenue growth over the next year based on current trends, alongside a table that breaks down expected expenses by department. Having this information in one place makes it easier for decision-makers to assess the company's financial health and plan for the future.

One of the most powerful aspects of Claude Artifact is its ability to create interactive dashboards. Unlike traditional business intelligence tools that offer static reports, Claude Artifact dashboards are dynamic, allowing users to explore the data in real-time. For example, in a meeting with senior leadership, you might start by presenting an overview of the company's sales performance. As questions arise, you can drill down into specific data points, such as regional performance or customer segments, to provide more detailed answers. The interactive nature of the dashboard allows for a more engaging and informative presentation, helping decision-makers to understand the data more fully and make better-informed choices.

This brings us to one of the most compelling use cases for a business intelligence dashboard built with Claude Artifact: replacing traditional PowerPoint slides in presentations. PowerPoint has long been the standard tool for business presentations, but it has its limitations. Static slides can quickly become outdated, and they don't allow for much flexibility when questions or new insights emerge during a meeting. By contrast, an interactive business intelligence dashboard provides a dynamic alternative that can adapt to the flow of the conversation.

Let's consider a real-world example. Imagine you're presenting quarterly sales results to the executive team. Instead of a PowerPoint deck filled with static charts and tables, you bring up an interactive dashboard built with Claude Artifact. As you go through the presentation, you can click on different elements of the dashboard to dive deeper into the data. If a question comes up about how a specific product performed in the last month, you can quickly pull up that data in real-time. If someone asks for more detail on market share in a particular region, you can zoom in on that part of the dashboard and explore the insights together. This level of interactivity not only keeps the audience engaged but also ensures that the presentation is more informative and valuable.

In this case study, the interactive dashboard essentially replaces the need for traditional slides. It offers a more flexible, data-rich approach to presentations, making it easier to convey complex information and respond to questions in real-time. This shift from static presentations to dynamic, interactive dashboards represents a significant advancement in how business intelligence is communicated within organizations.

In conclusion, Claude Artifact's ability to create business intelligence dashboards is a game-changer for organizations looking to make data-driven decisions. By transforming raw data into actionable insights, these dashboards provide a clear, concise view of key performance metrics, allowing businesses to stay ahead of the competition. Whether you're tracking sales performance, analyzing market share, or forecasting financial outcomes, Claude Artifact offers the tools needed to visualize and interpret your data with ease. And with its interactive capabilities, it even has the potential to revolutionize how presentations are delivered, replacing traditional slides with a more engaging and informative format.

Chapter 5: Real-Time Interactive Social Media Analyzer

- **Monitoring Sentiment on Social Media**: How to use Claude Artifact to track positive, negative, and neutral sentiments from different social media platforms.
- **Example: Tracking YouTube Comments**: A use case of how the author tracks YouTube comments using the social media sentiment analyzer.
- **Customizing Data for Deeper Insights**: Explanation of how the tool can be modified to track specific data points or posts.

Social media has become a powerful tool for understanding public opinion, brand perception, and customer feedback. The real-time nature of platforms like Twitter, YouTube, and Facebook gives businesses and individuals unprecedented access to what people are saying about their products, services, and even personal brands. However, with the overwhelming volume of content generated on social media daily, it can be difficult to manually track and analyze all relevant conversations. This is where Claude Artifact comes in as a game-changer, offering a real-time interactive social media analyzer that not only monitors sentiment but also provides actionable insights from social media data.

Sentiment analysis is one of the key features of Claude Artifact's social media monitoring tool. The tool works by automatically categorizing social media content into positive, negative, or neutral sentiments. Whether it's a tweet, a YouTube comment, or a Facebook post, Claude Artifact can scan the text, detect the emotion behind the words, and generate insights that reveal how people feel about a particular topic, brand, or person. This allows businesses to stay on top of their online reputation, address customer concerns in real-time, and capitalize on positive feedback to further engage their audience.

Let's imagine you're managing a brand that just launched a new product. As you monitor the online buzz, you notice a surge of mentions on social media. Instead of going through each post manually, Claude Artifact can provide an instant overview of the sentiment surrounding your product launch. You can see a breakdown of how many posts are positive, how many are negative, and how many are neutral. results by platform, date, or even by specific keywords, helping you to uncover more nuanced insights. For example, if you're monitoring a marketing campaign across multiple social media platforms, you can see how sentiment varies between Twitter, Instagram, and YouTube. This might reveal that while your campaign is performing well on Twitter, the reception on YouTube is less favorable. With this insight, you can adjust your strategy to target different platforms more effectively.

Let's consider a specific example of how this tool could be used in real-time. Say you're a content creator with a large following on YouTube, and you want to keep track of how viewers are reacting to your latest video. You could set up Claude Artifact to monitor the comments section of that particular video. The tool would analyze each comment and classify it according to sentiment, giving you an instant snapshot of how your audience is responding. If there's a sudden spike in negative comments, you'll be able to identify the source of dissatisfaction immediately, whether it's an issue with the video content itself, a controversial topic, or technical problems with the upload.

In this scenario, Claude Artifact provides a real-time sentiment report, showing the overall percentage of positive, negative, and neutral comments. Beyond this, you can also drill down into specific comments to see what people are saying in more detail. You might discover that while some negative comments are about technical issues (like video quality or buffering problems), others might provide valuable feedback on the content itself, suggesting ways to improve future videos. Armed with this knowledge, you can engage with your audience directly, addressing concerns and thanking those who offered constructive criticism.

The real power of Claude Artifact's social media analyzer comes from its ability to customize data tracking to fit your specific needs. You don't have to settle for generic sentiment analysis; instead, you can modify the tool to track the exact data points that matter to you. For example, if you're interested in tracking how your brand is being discussed during a particular event or campaign, you can set up custom filters to monitor only the posts that mention specific hashtags or keywords. This can be especially useful for tracking the success of marketing campaigns, where you might want to analyze how many people are talking about your campaign and whether their sentiment is positive or negative.

Customization goes beyond just keyword tracking. You can also set the tool to track specific users or influencers to see how their posts are influencing the overall sentiment. For instance, if a popular influencer posts about your brand, you can use Claude Artifact to monitor the immediate impact of that post on your brand's sentiment. You might find that the influencer's endorsement leads to a surge of positive sentiment, driving new customers to your product. Alternatively, if the influencer posts a critical review, you can track how that affects the sentiment and take steps to mitigate any potential damage to your reputation.

Claude Artifact also offers the ability to track sentiment over time, providing insights into how public opinion changes as a campaign progresses or as new developments occur. For example, if you're running a multi-phase marketing campaign, you can monitor how sentiment shifts from the initial launch to later stages of the campaign. This allows you to adjust your strategy in real-time, ensuring that you're always responding to the latest trends and feedback. If you notice that sentiment is starting to decline after the initial excitement wears off, you can introduce new content or promotions to re-engage your audience and keep the momentum going.

One of the most valuable aspects of Claude Artifact's social media analyzer is its ability to provide actionable insights. It's not just about tracking sentiment for the sake of knowing what people are saying; it's about using that data to make better decisions. For businesses, this means being able to respond to customer feedback in real-time, improve products or services based on what customers are saying, and capitalize on positive sentiment to build brand loyalty. For content creators and influencers, it means staying connected with your audience, understanding what they love about your content, and making adjustments to ensure that you're always delivering value.

In the case of tracking YouTube comments, for example, the data provided by Claude Artifact can help content creators to refine their approach to future videos. If a particular video receives a lot of positive feedback about its format or content style, the creator can use that insight to produce more videos in a similar vein. On the other hand, if viewers express confusion or dissatisfaction with certain aspects of the video, the creator can take that feedback on board and make improvements for future uploads. This not only helps to keep the audience engaged but also fosters a sense of community, as viewers feel that their opinions are being heard and valued.

To summarize, Claude Artifact's real-time interactive social media analyzer is an incredibly powerful tool for tracking sentiment and gaining deeper insights from social media platforms.

By categorizing posts into positive, negative, or neutral sentiments, the tool provides users with a clear understanding of how their brand or content is being perceived online. With its customizable features, users can tailor the tool to track specific data points, influencers, or timeframes, making it a highly flexible solution for businesses and content creators alike. Whether you're monitoring a brand's reputation, analyzing the success of a marketing campaign, or keeping track of YouTube comments,

Claude Artifact offers the real-time insights needed to stay ahead of the curve and make data-driven decisions.

Chapter 6: Games and Learning Tools with Claude Artifact

- **Building Simple Educational Games**: How to create interactive games, such as quizzes and true/false games, using Claude Artifact.
- **Case Study: Teaching Large Language Models with Games**: Detailed example of building an educational game that tests knowledge of large language models.
- **Expanding Games into Interactive Lessons**: Walkthrough of turning PowerPoint files into interactive lessons and quizzes, with a focus on educational use cases.

The integration of interactive technology into education has transformed how we approach learning. Claude Artifact offers educators and creators a unique opportunity to build engaging learning tools, such as educational games, quizzes, and interactive lessons, without needing extensive technical expertise. By leveraging this tool, anyone can create dynamic, engaging experiences that foster both enjoyment and learning. This chapter will explore how to use Claude Artifact for developing simple educational games, expanding these into interactive lessons, and a case study on using games to teach large language models.

Educational games serve as powerful learning aids because they promote active participation and engagement from learners. Instead of passively absorbing information, students can interact with the material, making the learning process more effective and enjoyable. Claude Artifact allows you to design simple, yet impactful games such as quizzes, true/false games, and multiple-choice questions with minimal effort. For instance, let's say you want to create a quiz for students learning about world geography. With Claude Artifact, you can simply input a set of questions and prompts, and the tool will generate an interactive quiz that students can play online. The quiz can feature different types of questions, ranging from identifying countries on a map to answering questions about capitals and landmarks.

By gamifying educational content, students are more likely to retain information and remain motivated to continue learning. Claude Artifact also makes it easy to adjust the difficulty level, ensuring that learners of all ages and abilities can participate. For example, you might design a quiz for younger students with simpler, multiple-choice questions, while more advanced students could be challenged with a mix of multiple-choice and open-ended questions.

The interactive nature of these games allows learners to receive instant feedback, reinforcing correct answers and guiding them through areas where they may need improvement.

Moving beyond simple quizzes, Claude Artifact offers the ability to create true/false games as well. These types of games can be particularly useful in testing quick recall of facts or concepts.

Let's say you're a science teacher looking to create a true/false game about animal biology. With Claude Artifact, you can input statements like "Penguins are mammals" or "Whales breathe through gills," and the tool will build an interactive game where students must determine whether each statement is true or false. This simple game format encourages students to think critically and quickly, making it a great tool for reinforcing foundational knowledge.

One of the standout features of Claude Artifact is how it allows users to take these simple games and expand them into full-fledged interactive lessons. For example, if you have a PowerPoint presentation on the solar system, you can upload it into Claude Artifact and turn it into an interactive lesson with quizzes, videos, and even drag-and-drop activities. Instead of students passively flipping through slides, they can engage with the content by answering questions, watching videos that explain key concepts, and completing activities that test their understanding of the material. This transforms what might otherwise be a static presentation into a dynamic learning experience.

Imagine a science teacher converting their PowerPoint presentation on the water cycle into an interactive lesson. Instead of students merely reading about evaporation, condensation, and precipitation, they can be prompted to match terms to their correct definitions or complete a diagram of the water cycle by dragging and dropping the correct labels. This level of interactivity ensures that students are not just absorbing the information but actively engaging with it, which enhances both retention and understanding.

A particularly compelling use case for Claude Artifact is in teaching complex subjects such as large language models. These models, which power everything from chatbots to search engines, can be challenging to explain in a way that is both engaging and understandable. However, by using Claude Artifact to build educational games, the material can be presented in a way that is more accessible to learners.

For instance, let's say you want to build an educational game that tests students' knowledge of how large language models work. You could create a game that prompts students with questions like "What is a neural network?" or "How does a language model predict the next word in a sentence?" Players could answer multiple-choice questions, complete sentences by choosing the correct word, or even simulate a conversation with a chatbot powered by a language model. This approach gamifies the learning process, making complex subjects more approachable and easier to digest.

A case study in this area could involve building a game that tests a student's understanding of large language models by using various levels of difficulty. In the beginner stages, players might be asked simple questions like "What does AI stand for?" As they progress through the levels, the questions become more complex, such as asking students to identify different types of neural networks or explain the process of backpropagation. By the final level, players could be tasked with diagnosing why a language model might produce incorrect outputs, applying the concepts they've learned throughout the game.

This method of teaching through games not only helps students grasp difficult concepts but also allows them to learn in a fun, interactive environment. Educational games built using Claude Artifact can be customized to suit various topics and difficulty levels, making them useful for a wide range of subjects, from science and mathematics to language arts and history.

Additionally, Claude Artifact's ability to transform traditional PowerPoint presentations into interactive lessons extends beyond the classroom. Corporate trainers, for example, could use the tool to create interactive modules for employee training. Instead of presenting static slides on company policies or product training, trainers can turn these presentations into interactive sessions where employees must complete quizzes, answer questions, or participate in simulations that test their understanding of the material. This not only makes the training more engaging but also ensures that employees are actively learning and retaining the information.

For example, a business might use Claude Artifact to create an interactive lesson on cybersecurity awareness. Employees could be presented with scenarios, such as identifying phishing emails or selecting the correct response to a potential data breach. By turning this into a game-like experience, employees are more likely to engage with the material and remember it when real-world situations arise.

Furthermore, educators who teach online courses can benefit from using Claude Artifact to create interactive lessons that mimic the traditional classroom experience. Instead of just reading through course material or watching lectures, students can participate in interactive activities, such as answering quiz questions or completing assignments directly within the platform. This fosters a more engaging online learning experience, ensuring that students stay motivated and actively participate in their own learning process.

In summary, Claude Artifact offers a powerful platform for creating educational games and interactive lessons that can enhance learning experiences in both traditional and non-traditional settings. Whether you're building a simple quiz, a true/false game, or an interactive lesson from a PowerPoint presentation, the tool makes it easy to design engaging, interactive content.

By leveraging the power of interactivity, learners are more likely to retain information, stay engaged, and develop a deeper understanding of the material. The case study of using games to teach large language models illustrates the potential for using Claude Artifact to make even the most complex subjects accessible and engaging. With Claude Artifact, the possibilities for enhancing education through interactive tools are virtually limitless.

Chapter 7: Advanced Features and Custom Dashboards

- **Creating Competitor Dashboards**: How to take screenshots of competitor websites and turn them into interactive dashboards.
- **Use Case: Top 10 YouTube Channels Dashboard**: A real-world example where the author compares popular YouTube channels using a competitor dashboard.
- **Advanced Use Cases for Business and Market Analysis**: Explanation of how these dashboards can be customized for business intelligence.

Claude Artifact offers a range of advanced features that elevate the process of creating interactive dashboards, making it not just a tool for basic applications, but a versatile solution for in-depth business analysis, competitive intelligence, and market monitoring. One of the most impactful uses of this tool lies in its ability to transform screenshots into fully functional dashboards that allow for real-time interaction and data-driven insights. This chapter explores how users can create competitor dashboards, focusing on a compelling use case involving the top 10 YouTube channels, and the broader application of these dashboards for business and market analysis.

Competitor analysis is a key component of any business strategy, and Claude Artifact's ability to convert screenshots into dashboards simplifies this complex process. By taking screenshots of competitor websites or online profiles, users can feed these images into Claude Artifact, which in turn transforms them into interactive dashboards. Imagine a scenario where a digital marketing firm wants to track its competitors' online activities. Instead of manually sifting through each competitor's website for updates, the firm can take a series of screenshots, input them into Claude

Artifact, and instantly generate a dashboard that consolidates the data, showing key metrics such as traffic, product listings, and pricing changes in real time.

This process offers a massive time-saving advantage. Traditional methods of competitor analysis might involve multiple software tools, data collection processes, and manual labor. But Claude Artifact allows users to streamline these tasks by automating much of the data organization, sorting it into easy-to-navigate dashboards. The interactivity provided by these dashboards ensures that data is not just displayed but can be explored dynamically. Users can filter information, zoom in on key metrics, and even cross-reference data points across multiple competitors, all within one seamless interface.

A standout example of how these dashboards can be applied is in the realm of social media analysis. Let's take a closer look at a use case that demonstrates the power of Claude Artifact in action—creating a competitor dashboard for the top 10 YouTube channels. In this example, we explore how the author utilizes Claude Artifact to compare some of the most popular YouTube channels by tracking subscriber growth, view counts, and content engagement metrics.

Imagine an influencer marketing agency tasked with analyzing the top 10 YouTube channels in a specific niche, say tech reviews. The agency's goal is to identify which channels are seeing the fastest growth and highest engagement rates. By gathering screenshots of the channels' analytics pages, including subscriber numbers, average views per video, and user comments, Claude Artifact can convert this static data into an interactive dashboard. The resulting dashboard allows the agency to easily compare each channel's performance over time, tracking metrics like daily subscriber increases, video engagement (likes, comments, and shares), and video release schedules.

For example, the dashboard might reveal that one particular channel consistently experiences a spike in subscribers after posting long-form content, while another channel's viewership surges when short, 5-minute videos are released more frequently. This insight allows the agency to make informed decisions on which channels to partner with for promotional campaigns, tailoring their strategies to the patterns discovered through Claude Artifact's competitor dashboard.

Moreover, the dashboard created with Claude Artifact can also help in tracking audience sentiment. By incorporating social media sentiment analysis into the dashboard, the agency can monitor how the audiences of these YouTube channels are responding to the content. Is the overall sentiment positive or negative? Which types of content generate the most excitement, and which topics lead to disengagement? Having this level of detailed insight gives the agency a significant competitive edge, as they can now base their decisions on concrete data rather than guesswork.

Beyond YouTube and social media analysis, the advanced features of Claude Artifact are invaluable in broader business and market analysis. With the ability to customize dashboards to specific business needs, organizations can harness this tool for a wide range of analytical tasks, from tracking sales performance to market share comparisons. Businesses can take screenshots of competitor product listings, market share reports, or financial forecasts, and Claude Artifact will turn these images into interactive data visualizations.

Let's say a retail company wants to track its market position relative to competitors in terms of pricing strategy, product variety, and customer feedback. By feeding Claude Artifact with screenshots of competitors' e-commerce platforms and customer reviews, the company can generate a competitor dashboard that visualizes pricing trends, product offerings, and overall customer sentiment. This allows decision-makers to quickly identify where their competitors are excelling or falling behind. For example, the dashboard might show that one competitor consistently offers lower prices but receives negative feedback on product quality, while another competitor excels in customer satisfaction but struggles with stock availability. Armed with this knowledge, the company can adjust its own strategies to balance pricing and quality or improve inventory management to stay competitive.

Another advanced use case for Claude Artifact's dashboards is in financial market analysis. Investment firms, for instance, could use the tool to monitor stock performance, quarterly earnings reports, and industry news. Screenshots of financial statements, stock market charts, and analyst reports can be fed into Claude Artifact to build a comprehensive dashboard that tracks the performance of specific stocks, sectors, or even entire markets. Investors can use the interactive features of the dashboard to filter by stock performance over specific time periods, compare growth rates across companies, and track financial news that may impact stock prices.

In this context, imagine a hedge fund using Claude Artifact to create a dashboard that tracks the stock performance of the top 50 tech companies. Screenshots from financial news websites, stock tracking platforms, and earnings reports are all integrated into a single interactive dashboard. The hedge fund managers can then use this tool to monitor stock trends, compare the performance of companies within the same sector, and track key financial metrics like earnings per share (EPS) and price-to-earnings (P/E) ratios. With this information at their fingertips, they can make more informed investment decisions, timing their trades to capitalize on market opportunities.

These advanced use cases highlight just how powerful Claude Artifact can be in the realm of business intelligence. By transforming static screenshots into interactive, real-time data dashboards, users gain the ability to analyze vast amounts of information quickly and effectively. Whether you're tracking competitors, analyzing market trends, or monitoring social media sentiment, the advanced features of Claude Artifact make it an indispensable tool for modern businesses.

Furthermore, the flexibility offered by Claude Artifact's dashboards means they can be customized to fit the unique needs of any organization. Different industries and use cases may require different metrics to be tracked, and Claude Artifact's ability to adapt to these needs makes it a versatile solution for any business looking to enhance its data analysis capabilities. Whether you're a social media manager tracking influencer performance or a financial analyst monitoring stock markets, Claude Artifact gives you the power to turn raw data into actionable insights.

In conclusion, Claude Artifact's advanced features and custom dashboards open up new possibilities for businesses seeking to gain a competitive edge. By turning simple screenshots into fully interactive dashboards, users can save time, streamline their workflow, and derive meaningful insights from the data they collect. Whether you're analyzing YouTube channels, tracking competitors, or monitoring the financial markets, Claude Artifact provides the tools needed to succeed in today's data-driven world.

Chapter 8: Claude Artifact for Games and Fun

- **Creating a Snake Game**: Step-by-step guide to creating a basic Snake game with a single prompt.
- **Fun with Coding Without Code**: How Claude Artifact picks programming languages (like React) to build interactive applications without the need for users to learn code.
- **Expanding Simple Games**: Discussing how users can further develop and customize these games for more complexity.

Claude Artifact opens up an intriguing world where games can be created and customized effortlessly without the need to dive into complex coding. Imagine being able to generate an interactive game, like the classic Snake, by simply entering a prompt. This is where the real magic of Claude Artifact lies—its ability to take basic inputs and transform them into fully functional applications, even games, that offer endless possibilities for both entertainment and learning. Let's explore how this tool can be harnessed to create fun experiences, starting with the development of a Snake game and expanding into more complex game designs, all without writing a single line of code.

The process of creating a Snake game with Claude Artifact is surprisingly simple yet fascinating. For those unfamiliar with the classic Snake game, it involves controlling a line (or "snake") that grows in length as it consumes food, all while avoiding collisions with itself or the boundaries of the game. Traditionally, building such a game would require knowledge of a programming language, such as JavaScript or Python, and an understanding of basic game mechanics. However, with Claude Artifact, all it takes is a carefully worded prompt to bring this timeless game to life.

Imagine typing something as simple as, "Create a basic Snake game where the snake grows as it eats food, and the game ends if the snake hits the wall or itself." From there, Claude Artifact does all the heavy lifting—choosing the appropriate programming language, such as React or JavaScript, and generating the necessary code behind the scenes. Within moments, a functional Snake game is ready to play, and the user can immediately begin testing it out. What makes this experience even more exciting is how easily the game can be modified and expanded upon. For instance, users can add features like speed adjustments, different levels of difficulty, or even multiplayer options, all through simple prompts.

One of the key advantages of using Claude Artifact for game development is its ability to handle coding without requiring the user to learn programming languages. Traditionally, creating an interactive application or game would involve writing code, debugging errors, and understanding the intricacies of various languages. However, Claude Artifact bypasses these technical barriers by picking the right tools—whether it's React for interactive web apps or another framework—and seamlessly generating code in the background. This means that even individuals with no prior programming experience can create sophisticated applications and games simply by communicating what they want through prompts.

For example, a user could prompt Claude Artifact to "create a quiz game with three difficulty levels, where each correct answer earns points, and the game tracks the player's score." From there, the tool would automatically select the appropriate programming framework, generate the necessary components (such as the questions, scoring system, and difficulty levels), and produce a fully functional quiz game that can be played immediately. This ability to create complex, interactive applications without any coding knowledge not only makes the process accessible but also invites creativity. Users can push the boundaries of what's possible, experimenting with different game mechanics and features simply by adjusting their prompts.

But the fun doesn't stop at basic games like Snake or quizzes. Claude Artifact also provides the flexibility to expand and customize games, adding layers of complexity that make them more engaging and unique. Take the Snake game, for instance—once the basic version is generated, users can modify it by adding elements such as power-ups, obstacles, or even themed levels that challenge the player in new ways. Perhaps the user wants to create a space-themed version of Snake, where the snake is a spaceship that grows as it collects fuel, dodging asteroids instead of walls. With Claude Artifact, these creative ideas can be executed effortlessly through prompts, allowing for endless customization options.

Furthermore, users can also explore more advanced game designs, building upon the basic frameworks that Claude Artifact generates. Imagine turning a simple quiz game into a full-blown educational tool, complete with multimedia elements like videos and images, or integrating leaderboards and timed challenges to make the game more competitive. These expansions not only add depth to the gameplay but also make the games more engaging for different audiences, whether it's students learning new concepts or casual players looking for a fun distraction.

In addition to expanding existing games, Claude Artifact offers the ability to build entirely new types of games from scratch. Consider the popular genre of puzzle games—using Claude Artifact, users can create a variety of puzzles, from word searches and crosswords to more intricate logic puzzles. For example, a user might prompt the tool to "create a Sudoku game with three levels of difficulty, where the player can choose between easy, medium, or hard puzzles." The tool would then generate the Sudoku game, complete with a user-friendly interface and the appropriate logic for solving the puzzles. Additionally, the user could request features like hints or a timer, making the game more interactive and challenging.

Another exciting aspect of game creation with Claude Artifact is its potential for collaboration. Since the tool generates code behind the scenes, users with coding knowledge can take the generated code and further customize it manually if they choose to do so. This means that Claude Artifact can serve as a starting point for more advanced developers, providing them with a foundation upon which they can build more complex or specialized games. On the flip side, users without any coding experience can still create impressive games without ever needing to look at the underlying code.

One particularly interesting use case for Claude Artifact in the realm of game development is its ability to create educational games. These games, which are designed to teach concepts or skills in an interactive format, are becoming increasingly popular in both schools and online learning platforms. With Claude Artifact, users can easily generate educational games that reinforce learning in a fun and engaging way. For instance, a teacher could use Claude Artifact to create a geography quiz game, where students have to identify countries on a map, or a math game that challenges players to solve equations under time pressure. The tool's ability to create interactive, visually appealing games makes it an ideal solution for educators looking to incorporate gamification into their lessons.

Moreover, Claude Artifact's intuitive approach to game creation makes it accessible to a wide range of users, from hobbyists and educators to professional developers and businesses. Its flexibility allows for the creation of games for various purposes, whether it's a simple pastime, an educational tool, or even a marketing strategy. Businesses, for example, could use Claude Artifact to create branded games that engage customers and promote products or services. Imagine a coffee shop creating a custom puzzle game where players match different types of coffee beans, with rewards for high scores redeemable as discounts in-store. This type of interactive content not only entertains but also fosters customer loyalty and engagement.

In conclusion, Claude Artifact opens up a world of possibilities for creating games and interactive applications without the need for coding knowledge. Whether users are looking to build a classic Snake game, develop educational tools, or expand simple games into more complex experiences, Claude Artifact provides an accessible and powerful platform for turning ideas into reality.

Its ability to handle the coding behind the scenes, combined with the flexibility to customize and expand games, makes it an invaluable tool for anyone interested in game development, from beginners to experienced developers. Whether for fun, education, or business, the possibilities with Claude Artifact are truly endless, making it an exciting tool for the future of interactive content creation.

Chapter 9: Claude Projects: Maximizing Potential

- **What is Claude Projects?**: Overview of how Claude Projects combines with Claude Artifact for powerful results.
- **Building a Knowledge Base**: How to create a personal or business knowledge base by uploading PDFs or documents.
- **Advanced Instructions for Projects**: Providing more detailed instructions to Claude Artifact using the knowledge base feature.
- **Use Case: A Comprehensive Project for AI**: Example of combining Claude Projects and Artifact to create an AI-driven project for business applications.

Claude Projects represent a new frontier in maximizing the potential of Claude Artifact. While Claude Artifact focuses on generating immediate and functional outputs based on prompts, Claude Projects takes this a step further by allowing users to create more complex, integrated systems that combine different elements like documents, files, and data sources.

Imagine having a tool that not only generates web apps or visual dashboards but also consolidates vast amounts of information into one seamless knowledge base. This is where Claude Projects truly shines—by creating a space where users can upload PDFs, documents, or other content, and transform them into interactive, AI-driven systems that streamline workflows, improve productivity, and enable powerful insights.

At its core, Claude Projects is designed to work in tandem with Claude Artifact. It enables users to take their outputs from Artifact and place them within a broader context, integrating multiple layers of data or resources into a single project. This could be as simple as building a knowledge base for personal use, where documents, files, and web-based outputs are organized into a coherent system, or as complex as creating an AI-driven platform for a business to manage tasks, analyze trends, and make informed decisions.

Creating a knowledge base is one of the most valuable functions within Claude Projects. For anyone looking to manage large amounts of information—whether it's research, company data, or even personal notes—the knowledge base feature enables you to upload PDFs, documents, or even spreadsheets, which can then be sorted, searched, and used interactively. Claude Projects doesn't just store these files; it actively processes them, analyzing the content to make it easily accessible and usable.

For example, if you were to upload a series of PDFs on a specific topic, Claude Projects could summarize the key points, extract actionable data, and even create prompts for further exploration within Claude Artifact.

Consider a business scenario where you're managing numerous documents related to sales reports, market analyses, and customer feedback. By uploading all of these files into Claude Projects, you could create a dynamic knowledge base that allows you to search for specific trends, visualize data, or cross-reference different reports. You could ask Claude Artifact to generate a sales performance dashboard based on the uploaded data, providing you with real-time insights that are both interactive and tailored to your specific needs.

In essence, Claude Projects serves as a hub where all your information is organized and made actionable through the power of Claude Artifact's functionalities.

What makes Claude Projects especially powerful is the ability to provide advanced instructions that guide how Claude Artifact interacts with the uploaded files. For instance, instead of just uploading a series of documents and passively waiting for outputs, users can provide detailed instructions on how to process the content.

This could involve specifying which sections of a PDF are most relevant for analysis, identifying key themes in a document, or directing Claude Artifact to create specific outputs (such as visual reports or web applications) based on the data. By refining the instructions, users can achieve highly customized results that cater to their precise needs.

Imagine you're running a business project that requires an analysis of market competition. You upload a series of competitor reports, financial statements, and customer reviews into Claude Projects. From there, you instruct Claude Artifact to extract relevant data points (such as competitor pricing strategies, sales figures, and consumer sentiment), generate interactive charts that visualize market trends, and create a competitor dashboard that updates in real-time. This level of detail and customization empowers users to take full advantage of Claude Projects' capabilities, ensuring that the outputs are not only relevant but also strategically aligned with business goals.

A prime example of combining Claude Projects and Claude Artifact for a comprehensive project involves creating an AI-driven system for business applications. Let's consider the example of developing an AI-powered assistant for managing a company's customer relationship management (CRM) system. By uploading a variety of documents—such as customer feedback reports, sales data, and product reviews—into Claude Projects, you can build a centralized knowledge base that the AI assistant can access and analyze.

The next step would be to instruct Claude Artifact to create specific outputs based on the uploaded data. For instance, the AI assistant could track customer sentiment over time by analyzing customer feedback, create visual charts that show sales performance in relation to product reviews, and even generate reports that identify potential areas for improvement based on consumer feedback trends. This AI-driven project would allow the business to make more informed decisions, optimize customer engagement strategies, and improve overall performance—all powered by the combination of Claude Projects and Artifact.

What sets this approach apart is the ability to continually update and expand the project over time. As new documents, data points, or customer feedback become available, they can be seamlessly integrated into the existing knowledge base, ensuring that the AI assistant remains up-to-date and relevant. This dynamic nature makes Claude Projects particularly well-suited for businesses that operate in fast-moving industries, where real-time insights and the ability to adapt quickly can be the difference between success and failure.

Moreover, the use cases for Claude Projects extend beyond just business applications. Educational institutions, for instance, could use it to create comprehensive learning platforms where students and educators alike can access a wealth of knowledge through an interactive interface. A professor could upload lecture notes, research papers, and study guides into a knowledge base, and then use Claude Artifact to generate quizzes, visual aids, or even interactive lessons that engage students in new and creative ways.

The result is a more immersive and effective learning experience, powered by AI and customized to the needs of both educators and students.

In the realm of personal projects, Claude Projects offers an exciting opportunity for individuals to create customized knowledge systems. Imagine using the tool to organize your personal notes, research materials, and ideas into an easily searchable and interactive format. Whether you're writing a book, working on a research project, or simply organizing your thoughts, Claude Projects provides the structure and tools necessary to transform scattered information into a coherent, actionable system.

For instance, a writer working on a novel could upload research notes, character descriptions, and plot outlines into Claude Projects. The tool could then analyze this information, identify key themes, and suggest ways to develop the story further. Similarly, a researcher could use Claude Projects to create a personal knowledge base that organizes academic papers, research findings, and experimental data, while Claude Artifact generates summaries, visual representations, and insights based on the uploaded content.

The versatility of Claude Projects and Claude Artifact, when combined, offers limitless possibilities for innovation. Whether it's in the realm of business, education, or personal creativity, the ability to organize, process, and act on vast amounts of information through AI-driven systems is transformative.

Claude Projects empowers users to build complex systems that not only store and manage data but also generate actionable insights and outputs that drive progress and success. It's a tool for those who want to maximize the potential of their ideas and projects, leveraging the power of AI to make the impossible achievable.

As we continue to explore the capabilities of Claude Projects, it's clear that this tool, in combination with Claude Artifact, represents a major step forward in how we manage, process, and interact with information. It simplifies complex tasks, enhances productivity, and opens up new possibilities for innovation in ways that were previously unimaginable. Whether you're building a knowledge base for personal use or developing an AI-driven project for a business, Claude Projects provides the structure and tools needed to take your ideas to the next level.

Chapter 10: How Claude Artifact Will Change Your Workflow

- **Why AI Tools are the Future of Productivity**: An analysis of how Claude Artifact and similar tools are reshaping industries.
- **The Benefits of Simplified AI Solutions**: Highlighting the ease of use for non-coders and how it enhances creativity and productivity.
- **The Road Ahead for AI Development**: Future prospects of AI tools like Claude Artifact and how they can impact different sectors.

Artificial Intelligence (AI) tools are rapidly changing the landscape of productivity, and Claude Artifact is at the forefront of this transformation. Imagine a world where time-consuming tasks, complex data analysis, and creative processes that once required hours of manual effort can now be handled in minutes with the help of intelligent automation. This is no longer a distant possibility but an immediate reality, as AI tools like Claude Artifact become more accessible and user-friendly, reshaping industries and workflows in profound ways.

At the core of Claude Artifact's innovation is its ability to offer highly advanced AI-powered solutions without the need for coding expertise. For decades, the integration of AI into business processes was limited to those with specialized technical knowledge, but now, anyone can harness the power of AI. This democratization of technology opens up new possibilities for individuals and organizations alike.

Suddenly, tasks that would have required a dedicated IT team or expert consultants can be managed by anyone with a basic understanding of how to interact with the platform. The barriers to entry have been lowered, empowering users to take control of their own productivity in ways they never thought possible.

One of the most compelling aspects of Claude Artifact is its ability to simplify workflows. Whether it's generating web apps from screenshots, building visual dashboards from raw data, or even creating educational tools with a single prompt, Claude Artifact takes complex tasks and makes them accessible to everyone. For non-coders, this is a game-changer. No longer is there a need to invest in expensive development resources or undergo months of training to build a functional app or dashboard.

Instead, users can focus on the creativity and strategy behind their projects, while Claude Artifact handles the technical execution. This shift allows people to tap into their full potential, moving beyond the limitations of their technical expertise and diving straight into innovation.

Take, for example, the process of creating a sales dashboard. In the past, this might have required a team of analysts to sift through large datasets, then a designer to turn that data into visually appealing charts, and finally a developer to build the dashboard itself.

With Claude Artifact, a single person can accomplish all of this within minutes. Simply upload the relevant data, provide a few instructions, and the AI does the rest. It organizes the information, builds the visualizations, and even allows for interactivity, so users can engage with the data in real-time. This level of simplicity doesn't just save time—it completely redefines the role of individuals within organizations, giving them more autonomy and enabling them to focus on high-level strategy and decision-making.

What's even more exciting about tools like Claude Artifact is the potential they hold for the future of work. As AI continues to evolve, the possibilities are endless. Already, we are seeing how these tools can be applied across industries—from business intelligence and marketing to education and entertainment.

In sectors like healthcare, AI tools can assist in analyzing medical records, generating treatment plans, or even predicting patient outcomes based on historical data. In the legal field, AI is being used to sift through thousands of documents in seconds, saving lawyers countless hours of manual review. And in the creative industries, AI is helping designers, writers, and artists to bring their visions to life more quickly and with fewer technical hurdles.

One of the key advantages of Claude Artifact is that it encourages creative problem-solving. Because the tool is so intuitive and user-friendly, users are not constrained by the technical complexities that often come with traditional software solutions. Instead, they are free to experiment, iterate, and push the boundaries of what's possible. This leads to innovation at a pace that was previously unimaginable. Whether it's a small business owner creating their first web app, or a data analyst building a sophisticated dashboard for a Fortune 500 company, the ability to generate results quickly allows users to iterate and improve their projects in real-time. This fosters a culture of continuous improvement and agility, where ideas can be tested, refined, and implemented in rapid succession.

Looking ahead, the road for AI development appears to be wide open, and Claude Artifact is poised to play a major role in shaping that future. As AI tools become more sophisticated, they will likely begin to anticipate user needs even more accurately, making recommendations and providing solutions before the user even knows what to ask for. The integration of natural language processing, machine learning, and predictive analytics will enable these tools to become not just assistants, but true collaborators in the creative and decision-making processes. Imagine an AI tool that can analyze your company's entire market landscape, predict trends, and offer actionable insights before you even ask the question. This level of proactive intelligence could redefine how businesses operate and compete in a global marketplace.

Moreover, as AI tools like Claude Artifact become more widely adopted, we are likely to see a shift in how entire industries approach productivity. The ability to automate routine tasks will free up employees to focus on more strategic, high-impact work. For example, instead of spending hours on data entry or manual report generation, employees will have more time to engage in creative problem-solving, develop new products, or focus on customer engagement. This shift will lead to more innovation, as organizations will be able to allocate more resources to the areas that truly drive growth and differentiation.

In fact, we're already seeing the early signs of this transformation. Forward-thinking companies are embracing AI not as a replacement for human workers but as a tool that enhances their capabilities. The focus is shifting from mundane, repetitive tasks to the kind of work that requires critical thinking, empathy, and creativity—areas where humans excel. By leveraging AI to handle the technical aspects, organizations can unlock the full potential of their workforce, allowing employees to focus on what truly matters.

The future prospects for AI tools like Claude Artifact are not just confined to business and industry. In education, AI has the potential to revolutionize how we learn and teach. Already, we are seeing AI-powered platforms that can tailor learning experiences to individual students, adapting lessons based on their strengths, weaknesses, and learning styles. With Claude Artifact, educators can create interactive lessons, build quizzes, and develop educational games without needing any programming skills. This accessibility opens up new opportunities for schools, teachers, and students to engage with technology in ways that were previously out of reach.

In entertainment, AI tools are helping to democratize creativity. Musicians, filmmakers, and writers can use AI to enhance their creative processes, generate new ideas, or even produce complete works of art. Claude Artifact, with its ability to generate apps and interactive content, provides artists and creators with a powerful new medium for expression. As AI continues to evolve, we may even see the emergence of entirely new art forms, where human creativity and AI-driven technology work hand in hand to produce experiences that are immersive, dynamic, and truly one-of-a-kind.

The benefits of simplified AI solutions like Claude Artifact go beyond just saving time or reducing costs. They represent a paradigm shift in how we think about work, creativity, and productivity. By making advanced technology accessible to everyone, regardless of their technical background, these tools are empowering individuals and organizations to achieve more than they ever thought possible. The future is bright, and with AI tools like Claude Artifact, we are just beginning to scratch the surface of what's possible.

As we move forward, the key to unlocking the full potential of AI will be in how we choose to embrace and integrate these tools into our daily lives. The road ahead is filled with opportunities, and for those who are willing to adapt and innovate, the possibilities are limitless. Whether you're a business leader looking to streamline operations, a creative professional seeking to push the boundaries of your art, or an educator working to inspire the next generation of learners, Claude Artifact offers a glimpse into a future where technology and human ingenuity come together to create something truly extraordinary.

CONCLUSION

- **Final Thoughts on Claude Artifact's Impact**: Summing up the importance of the tool in both personal and professional contexts.
- Encouraging Readers to Experiment with AI: Inviting readers to explore and experiment with Claude Artifact based on the examples provided.
- The Future of AI in Everyday Life: Concluding remarks on the growing role of AI and the opportunities it brings.

As we draw to a close, it's essential to reflect on the profound impact Claude Artifact has made, not only in professional settings but in personal contexts as well. This tool represents a significant leap forward in the realm of artificial intelligence, offering unprecedented access to advanced functionalities that were once the exclusive domain of technical experts. By democratizing access to these powerful capabilities, Claude Artifact is redefining how we approach both everyday tasks and complex projects.

Claude Artifact's impact is far-reaching. In the professional world, it simplifies and streamlines processes that were traditionally cumbersome and time-consuming. The ability to create interactive dashboards, build applications from screenshots, and generate visual charts without a deep technical background has opened new avenues for productivity and creativity. Businesses can now leverage these tools to make informed decisions based on real-time data, create engaging presentations, and enhance their operational efficiency. The implications are enormous, allowing teams to focus on strategic initiatives rather than getting bogged down by technical details.

On a personal level, Claude Artifact empowers individuals to explore and realize their own creative and analytical projects. Whether it's developing a simple to-do list app, crafting a business intelligence dashboard, or even designing an educational game, users are no longer constrained by their coding abilities.

This newfound freedom to innovate fosters a sense of empowerment and possibility, enabling individuals to turn their ideas into tangible results with remarkable ease. The accessibility of such powerful tools encourages a more engaged and proactive approach to personal and professional challenges.

As we've seen throughout this book, Claude Artifact is not just about performing specific tasks—it's about unlocking a new way of thinking about technology and its role in our lives. The examples and use cases presented here illustrate how this tool can be applied to a wide range of scenarios, from business analytics to interactive learning. By integrating AI into these processes, users are able to achieve results that were previously unattainable without extensive technical expertise.

Encouraging readers to experiment with AI is a natural extension of this exploration. Claude Artifact provides a unique opportunity to dive into the world of artificial intelligence without needing a deep technical background. The examples shared throughout this book serve as a starting point, but the true power of the tool lies in the ability to push boundaries and explore new possibilities. Don't be afraid to experiment—try out different prompts, build diverse applications, and see how Claude Artifact can enhance your own workflows and projects. The only limit is your imagination.

The future of AI in everyday life is bright and full of potential. As AI technology continues to evolve, tools like Claude Artifact will become even more integrated into our daily routines. We can anticipate a future where AI assists in a variety of tasks, from personal productivity to complex decision-making. The opportunities are vast, and the potential for innovation is limitless. Embracing these advancements will not only help individuals and businesses stay competitive but will also foster a culture of continuous improvement and creativity.

In conclusion, Claude Artifact stands as a testament to the transformative power of artificial intelligence. It symbolizes a shift towards a more inclusive and accessible approach to technology, where advanced tools are available to everyone, regardless of their technical skills. As you move forward, keep exploring and experimenting with AI, and stay curious about the possibilities it can offer.

The journey into the world of AI is just beginning, and with tools like Claude Artifact at your disposal, the future is not only promising but incredibly exciting.

www.ingramcontent.com/pod-product-compliance
Lightning Source LLC
Chambersburg PA
CBHW050319230526
45471CB00005B/2253